"The Get That... anyone wishin... today's high... helped me i... develop my spiritual self further."

Andy Hocking.

Alison's messages are always inspirational, uplifting, and enlightening...very often it seems the subject is exactly what I need at the time - and often provides answers to questions that I hadn't consciously asked. Alison is an amazingly gifted lady, and her channelled messages are truly helpful.

Janice ~ Staffs, United Kingdom

Alison's channelled messages are perfectly aligned, whenever I read them I feel like they have been written just for me! The down to earth soul guidance helps me connect with my true self and a sense of peacefulness.

Dr Anjela Heron ~ Wellbeing Mentor for children, New Zealand

Testimonials

I absolutely love the Get that Friday Feeling messages from Alison. They are so beautiful and full of inspiration. It is truely a blessing to recieve them and know how much we are loved. I usually read them on my phone and I have taken pictures of many of them which I reread and share with my family. Thank you Alison for sharing these wonderful messages, you have made Friday my favorite day of the week!

Linda Yakaitis ~ Conneticut, USA

Where to begin to describe the benefits of Alison's Friday Feeling Channelled Messages: uplifting, motivating and inspiring. With the day to day mantra and negative chatterbox that many people like myself suffer with its refreshing to read her weekly channelled messages to redirect myself to speak and act on a more loving and connected level. Thank you Alison for all you have taught me.

J Millar ~ Lisburn. Northern Ireland.

Angel Alison is an amazing woman and channels beautiful and much needed messages from the angels. Each of these messages feels as if it has been personally channeled directly for me.

Debbie Bolton ~ Scotland.

Get that
Friday Feeling

Angel Alison Ward

Get That *Friday Feeling*

Copyright © 2015 Alison Ward. All rights reserved.
ISBN - 978-1-907308-38-3

www.angelalisonward.guru

First Published in Great Britan by Compass Publishing 2015
In collaboration with Hearts of England Ltd

Designed by The Book Refinery Ltd

No part of this e-book shall be reproduced or transmitted in any form or by any means, electronic or mechanical, including photocopying, recording, or by any information retrieval system without written permission of the publisher.

Dear Reader, you may notice some spelling errors in these channellings. I'm often told to leave them as they are as they are original in orign ie via my channel. Remember the angelic realms use our words to express much more varied meanings. Eg *Selfish* isn't necessary a bad thing, it means you are focussing on your own self development. So let go of the feeling of being perfect and absorb with the LOVE they exude.

A *Guiding Light* Series

Introduction

Get That Friday Feeling is the latest book in the 'Guiding Light' series. It was born a few years ago. Here's the story from Angel Alison;

A few years back whilst considering investing in some PR help to get exposure for my work, I was given the idea to use my gift of channelling on a weekly basis; every Friday. We called it *'Get That Friday Feeling channelled messages'*.

I loved the idea as it was a way of sharing the gifts (as I call them) with the world. The messages always inspire, uplift and give wisdom for the reader but also for myself. They have become my teacher, mentor and guide. So as the gifts are shared with my LOVE, I also get a gift from them. I love win win situations!

There is another reason why I LOVE these gifts from the Universe. When we live our life aligned to our core values and beliefs and share our gifts with the world, we naturally become happier, more fulfilled and yes, even successful. More and more of us are realising we don't have to work Monday to Friday 9 to 5 to create magical lifestyles, typically aligned to Get That Friday Feeling. I'm hoping these messages will inspire YOU and YOUR life dear reader.

How to use this book

How do you use GTFF?

There are several ways to use the beautiful messages in GTFF.

Here are some suggestions;

Ground, centre and connect with your breath then simply ask the Angels and Universe, 'what message would you like me to hear today?' Then simply open the book to wherever you feel guided. Write the message down in today's journal entry and throughout

the day think back to the message and integrate it into your day. At the close of the day, reflect back and give your thanks and gratitude for the message and it's teachings.

2. Go to a significant date (if it's there, or the nearest date you can find) and read the message

for that birthday, anniversary or significant date. Again, write it down and reflect on what it's shown you at the close of day.

3. Have you a particular problem or niggle you need some insight or clarity with? if so ground, centre and connect then ask the angels and universe to choose the message that will assist you. Again write it down, remind yourself throughout the day and reflect on it at the close of day.

4. Randomly open the book and see what message 'pops' out, this is your very direct message for today or NOW!

Please use the messages to further your self development and connection, remember they were born out of LOVE from the angels and Universe via Angel Alison as a gift to YOU, to encourage you on your journey of life.

Receive them with LOVE, apply with LOVE and fly with LOVE.

Alison xx

Dedicated to...

I wish to dedicate this book to all my angels who always surround me with their LOVE and support and use me as a channel to inspire others.

I am eternally great-full!

To my angel on earth, Karen Ward (formerly McCarthy) you were THE ONE who inspired and encouraged me to write and carry on when life was oh so challenging. You were the one who reassured me when life got on top of me and challenges took over. I'm here, happy and fulfilled at sharing these words to inspire others.

Thank you for believing in me.

2nd July

"You leave with the attitude you become..."

21st September

"Dare to dream today.... Without effort or force. Wonderful developments will occur."

21st December

"Today's the day to join forces with your fellow man and enjoy the coming together of souls. You have waited for this day and now it's upon you celebrate,
release and accept the golden age.
Let go of fear and procrastination...now is the time..!"

1st February

"Today's a new beginning for you, take it with both hands and open your heart to change that will enhance you life. Practice tasks and past times that bring you joy and make your heart sing. Engage with those souls who *"see you"*, the real you and encourage you to grow with love. Surround yourself with colour and texture, bring nature into the home and walk amongst it in your free time.
Spend time alone and form a deep friendship with yourself,
speak slowly when speaking your truth.
Be silent... every day; even for a little while.
Notice the difference as you bring this discipline into your daily practice.
Remember we are close by..."

8th February

"This one is for YOU, yes you, you know who you are. Deny yourself no more, you are an amazing being, there is no one else quite like you so why hide your LIGHT. Now is your chance to shine, dare to dream and live in hope and belief. You have the power to transform and change as soon as you decide. We are so close, with you, guiding you, supporting you through your thoughts, dreams, coincidences and synchronicities so look up, aim high and get ready to fly!"

11th February

When the weather slows everything down, take time to enjoy this slower pace of life. Reflect on your thoughts, feelings and desires then simply state them out loud!
They may surprise you. xx

13th February

Go on. Do something new today...

8th March

"Welcome to today, a day where we ask you to explore the possibilities as you allow gratitude to truly spread throughout your day. Praise be that you have life and LOVE. Spread your LIGHT to your fellow man in your own unique ways; a smile, a wave or a helping hand. Remember we are always with you, if you need a reminder all you do is ask for a sign...then watch...
We LOVE YOU WHOLLY & COMPLETELY."

13th March

"Welcome to the world of wonder.
Of...embracing life
YOUR LIFE!
Now is the time
To push through those barriers of fears,
stubbornness, resistance, apathy and yes even laziness (we are human),
To co create the life you truly desire.
YOU have an array of speakers who have all stared their fears in the eyes and said
'take a hike'
Embrace this day, this is YOUR day,
the day YOU decide to take the step.
Now is the time!"

18th March

"Morning angels everywhere, the sun is shining so we ask you if your light is shining? Come on Shine your LIGHT today. We are with you helping you shine!"

22nd March

"It's time, time for action without delay or compromise. The equinox has awakened your inner self your soul awakening. Now is the time to bring fruit to your dreams and desires. Acknowledge your desires without fear of lack and limitations and watch them spring into shape.
Now IS the time."

5th April

"Who are YOU?" Do you know?
What relationship do you and YOU have?
Is it time to get to know the real YOU?
We know you, we love YOU and we accept YOU.
The world wishes to see the real YOU so come
on, it's time to explore and discover YOU."

19th April

"Welcome to the birth of your new day. I am here today to propose to you... 'ooh', I hear you say. (Angels have a fab sense of humour.)
My proposal is to start this day anew, clean and fresh. Wipe the slate clean of all previous days and approach this day with the zest and passion of a new born. Who will meet your needs today? who will be your nurturer? You? Or some wonderful earth angels? Embrace this feeling of newness without expectation. Live today in the new way and watch how your garden grows.... more to follow."

7th June

"Don't give up the fight, the passion, the trust and belief. All is well in your world, sometimes you just can't see it."
We LOVE YOU."

11th June

We believe in YOU!

14th June

"As you look skywards, what do you see? Angels in the clouds or a drizzly, grey sky. Your eyes and sight create your experiences in coalition with your mind. So if your sky is drizzly and grey today, why not change it into a glorious, blue sky, clear and light?"

5th July

It's 19 years since the day of my Awakening today, so time to reflect back over the last 19 years and count my blessings for being who I am today.
Thank you to everyone who has read
Awarded by Angels...
Bless you my angels xxxx

"Hello all, as you enjoy the sunshine breathe it in, deeply onto your lungs and fill your organs with the rays of the sun. Let this light fill you up so you may shine ever brighter."
Archangel Jophiel x

12th July

"It's not what you DO that makes you so special, it's what YOU are.
Just saying..."
Archangel Arial

LOVE IT!

19th July

We're a little later this week but you have not been forgotten.

"We are always with you, loving you, guiding you, prompting you asking you to nurture YOU! You are important, unique and special in every way, we love you totally and unconditionally. Can you feel it?"

26th July

"Be still and listen. Just for a few moments.
Listen to your heart and soul re connect.
Can you hear it? Silence!
See how it brings such peace. To you,
your environment and then observe the ripples
filter into your life, your thoughts,
feeling and all actions. Please do not deny
yourself the gift of silence.
It brings many gifts and creates limitless
opportunities."
Archangel Sandalphon

27th July

Love is the antidote! X

12th August

"It's time to state your dreams and desires.
Now is the time to make them happen.
Get out your Vision boards, write what it is you
truly desire, place it where you can see and
build up the energy..."

13th August

"Listen to your heart.
It's trying to tell you something.
It's close...
All that work is coming to fruition.
There is no shortage of LOVE,
opportunities and flow of money.
Stay close to your dream.
Believe in YOU; we do!"

How lovely xxx
Well I certainly do trust and believe so bring it on!
Thank you angels xxx

23rd August

"We are here listening to your every word,
feeling your every pain,
happiness, joy and sorrow. For many of you
are awakening to all that is;
the great wonder of the Universe.
We implore you to dig further, explore and
challenge your limiting beliefs. It is so much
vaster than you can imagine.
You are part of it, like a grain of sand on a long
beach. Each particle has its place and purpose -
creating part of the whole! All the more to be
mindful of every thought, action and practice as
YOU are part of the whole too!"

30th August

Get that Friday feeling has been influenced by hearing of a few relationship break ups this week so I asked for a message to help all those in a relationship that no longer serves them. I truly hope this gives you confirmation that you have made the right decision.

"Look into the eyes of the ONE you love. What do you see looking back at you?
Love and acceptance for who you are
or despair and pain?
You are living in the time of truth and acceptance. If your relationships does not have that as its foundation, it's not going to bear the weather of longevity! Be honest with yourself, demand more and accept that you *are* worth it."

6th September

Today's Get that Friday feeling is influenced by the sudden passing of one of our friends at The Holistic Hut in Rugelely. We're all thinking about Sarah Cornwall and her family today as they say farewell to Alison Cornwall.

"Farewell, not goodbye. Your loved ones are in safe hands as you grieve for your loss of their PHYSICAL presence. They are still with you in spirit and sound. Open and heighten your awareness to stay in contact with your dearly departed souls. They are now in peace and celebrating that their soul contracts been finalised and completed.
In other words, their work on earth is done.
They can now rest and be reunited with their soul families on their vibration. Fear not, they are still with you and will never leave you.
Life is for making memories, holding joy and laughter, so take this as an invitation to celebrate your life too as you say farewell to
a dear soul today."
Archangel Azrael.

18th September

"Calling all angels everywhere, I must share with you that I'm experiencing a wonderful time of manifesting or as I prefer to say *co creating*, I would love to share with you how; read *Bringing it Back to YOU!* for more info. Xx

27th September

We're feeling sad, after receiving hatemail today, so let's link in and see what the angels have to say for *'Get that Friday Feeling channelled message...'*

"Open your heart dear child and recognise not only their hate and betrayal but their fear and separation from the LIGHT! YOUR LIGHT IS SO STRONG AND BRIGHT that it hurts their eyes. They feel intimidated by your LOVE and commitment for life and its purpose.
What is the purpose of life we ask?
Simply to be the best person you can be, learn your lessons, open your heart and serve us through pure inspiration. You see when you are the person that knows his purpose, when you continue to shine your LIGHT, you naturally inspire others. Keep shining!"
Archangel Uriel

11th October

Get that Friday feeling is a little later for some of you today. I'm writing this in Prescott Arizona. Tomorrow I'll be heading off for a retreat in Sedona for 5 days.
Tell you all about it next week.
So what is today's message?

"Hello Dear Ones. We meet again. Open your hearts' your inner hearing vessel and listen to our words of LOVE & Wisdom. Today we wish to draw your attention to releasing judgement from your mind and soul. It is a natural human response and reaction to judge another person or situation. It's your way of assimilating the evident information then concluding what YOU see and hear. Remember your experiences in Your life are totally unique to YOU...NO ONE else has experienced them in the same way as you; through your eyes and ears. Can you now see how a misjudgement is formed? So we ask you...urge you to release judgements as soon as you become aware that you are in that process.

The cover of a book can often be misleading to the story inside! Do you understand today's lesson? Please do ask us any questions. You have our attention."

Hmm how very interesting. That channelling was the LIGHT COUNCIL who surround and guard our Earth. Very wise beings of LIGHT.
Any questions? Ask away....

1st November

Good Morning angels everywhere around the World! How are you today? Well I could burst with joy and excitement at all the wonderful things that are happening and our recent trip to Arizona in USA. A great testament to the fact that after dark times with hope and belief the sun rises again and the good times start happening so if you're in a 'dark place' at the moment, then believe! Believe it will get better, do things that you enjoy doing, laugh, move your body..anything to change that dark, stagnant energy that occurs when life becomes dark and scary.
Let's see what channelled message we're given today:

"Welcome dear ONES. We are here as always, in fact we have never left you. We are with you in your thoughts, dreams, ideas and often actions. Prompting you, nudging you to move in the best direction (for you!).

1st November cont'

When your life becomes darker bring in the LIGHT literally. Light = joy, love, laughter, truth and compassion... bring it in at every opportunity including physically lighting a candle, opening the blinds, adding even more LIGHT. You will become more acclimatised to LIGHT then the darkness in terms of fearful thoughts, (that lead to fear full actions) will have no place. They simply have no place in the light surroundings. Come on all it requires is a little effort to get out of that staid place of fear, dust off the fear dust and change the energy."

Remember, you are never, ever on your own, no matter what YOU think!
A reassuring thought eh!

8th November

Hello to all of you who tune in each week with an open heart and anticipation for the weekly message.

We are here today to say YOU are beautiful. Yes YOU, the person who is reading this. We LOVE you, accept you, honour you and wish to help you in all of your thoughts and actions.
Do not strive for perfection; there is no such thing. There is absolutely no need to compare yourself to another, they have blood running though their veins just like you, they have fears too just like you.
Embrace YOU in all aspects, grace the body you were given that houses your soul. Bring balance to your mind and emotions in your daily activities by moving your body, allowing it to rest, fuelling it with foods that suit you. Finally... breathe! A natural skill you were given that is quite often forgotten. It occurs naturally (of course), but in your rest times be mindful as you take a deep breath in, fill your lungs, hold it , then exhale.
These few breaths will bring you to centre and ultimately balance.

Til we meet next week.

15th November

Get that Friday feeling channelled message is being written in magical Venice today.

"Create your magical life by daring to dream. You are a wondrous child that is able to co create all that you desire...as soon as you get your head out of the way and learn to trust and surrender. The universe holds many gifts so why should YOU not receive them when others do?
Simply allow yourself to sit with YOU and create your desires first and foremost. Then trust, believe and surrender, leaving the rest to us."

Happy manifesting angels everywhere. See you next Friday. Ciao x

1st December

I wish to share my Vision with you; will you spare a few moments reading this please? xx

Ok I've decided to share my ultimate vision with you all since this is the time of festive greetings and festive beatings!
Yes you heard me right! There are many men and women out there who use the stresses and strains of this time of year to beat their so called loved ones.
My book *Awarded By Angels* describes my personal journey from being such a survivor, I know about the shame and the silence!
So here is my vision:

For *Awarded By Angels* and my next book *Bringing YOU back to YOU!* to sell millions of copies to enable me and my family to live a good life which we can pass on. The money raised from sales plus Im sure some very wealthy people contributing too will create a

1st December

charity that will own several homes around the UK, all decorated to a lovely standard; no shit holes! We will then rent these out to those in need of somewhere to live after leaving *'their situation'*. They will have a maximum of 2 years in their new home in which time they will get access to some great mentors who will share with them their own personal tools of transformation. With these new tools plus great people supporting them, they will realise they have choices. The help will include employment support so all in all a huge support network is needed for this Vision to be achieved. It's a vision made up of love and passion for all human beings to be free..from pain, violence and shame..

So what do you think? If you want to help in anyway, please do let me know.
With LOVE XXxx

2nd December

A little taster for you.
A quote from my next book
Bringing You back to YOU!"

"To return to YOU is a return to LOVE. True LOVE,
without limitations and expectations.
Give yourself the gift of LOVE and bring
you back to YOU!"

13th December

"Today is a day where we celebrate you.
We ask that you join us in our celebrations
and give your-self a day off from
harsh words and thoughts.
Buy yourself a gift in recognition of
all the kind acts you do for others;
that is our gift to you.
The money spent on you will return.
Thank yourself for allowing you to develop,
grow in awareness and become an even better
person. Give yourself the gift of food that your
body welcomes and applauds! Spend time with
those who make your heart sing and your belly
ache from laughter. We are the angels
surrounding you day and night urging you to
celebrate who you are. We do!"

20th December

Get That Friday Feeling is been channelled very early today; my angels and guides keep waking me up at 3am to write. My next book; Bringing You back to YOU! is now finished. To order your signed copy of Bringing You Back To YOU with your very own personal chanelled message from the angels, go to www.angelalisonward.guru
What have we in store for today?

"Morning angel lovers around the globe, how are you feeling today? In LOVE or in fear? We wish to remind you, that you have the power to change your thoughts and indeed your life! As soon as you align to LOVE the emotions move in alignment also. We know so many of you are hurting at this time of year and we ask you to join forces with people who LOVE and support you, they will buoy your faith
with their LOVE for you.

20th December cont'

If you feel there is no one out there who LOVES you, reach out to us, we are always here listening and trying to reach you through your thoughts, desires, dreams and senses.
Tell us your fears and hurts, better still write it all down in a letter and post it right back at you. Spend time in silence so we can give you gentle nudges of reassurance through your channel. Be open to receive our LOVE, it is ever present and everlasting. Believe and you will learn to trust dear lonely ones, believe."

Aah lovely. Hope it resonates and brings you peace dear reader. Xxx

23rd December

*So what's today's festive channelling?
Let's see;*

"Welcome once more, as you connect with the channellings you continue to open doors to greater love and assistance. Remember we are with you always. If you need our help simply call on us and tell us how we can help. Sometimes dear ones, the outcome may not be quite what you planned! We have access to the bigger picture; your bigger picture of life so trust us, we know what we're doing.

We would like you to practice mindfullness today. Bring your whole attention and love to all of your tasks, be truly present. You will notice the food tastes even nicer, the presents more beautifully wrapped, live today as if it's your last. Say thank you, I LOVE you and bless you. Notice how the vibration lifts. Finally sing 'til your heart sings with you and laugh 'til your belly aches."

Archangel Jophiel xx

27th December

*Get that Friday Feeling channelled message is here again, the last one of the year.
What have we got in store for us today?*

"Welcome dear ones, we hope you have enjoyed the celebrations. As you now prepare to leave this year behind, reflect and learn what has occurred in your life over the last twelve months. Many of you have taken great leaps of faith and trust. Well done, you have opened the doors to receiving so much more. Trust and belief are two main ingredients leading you to a happy and prosperous life. Let go of all your limitations as you discover what it is you truly desire, really allow your mind and soul to dream; then trust and believe. As you let go of the outcome to your desires, you create more of an energetic flow bringing them into your life without restriction. We would like to ask you to take this letting go of expectations into your 2014. See how your life is in flow, feel the stress disappear and see the smile stay firmly on your face.
Remember; we love you, wholly and unconditionally.
Yes YOU reading this."

Very wise words eh? xxx

3rd January

Welcome to today's Get That Friday Feeling; the first of the year. What have our beautiful guides got for us today?

"Welcome dear ones from around the world. You are an amazing and awesome sight. You are gifted and talented and that's just the beginning.
You are here to shine your LIGHT, in all that you do. Please do not let life's fears get the better of you. Take a leap of faith when your heart urges you, believe in you and others will follow. Remember procrastination is the ego's game to keep you separate from fulfilling your dreams!
This is the year of completion, finish what you have started and notice how LIGHTER you are. Go on we dare you."

10th January

Good Morning. Here is today's *Get That Friday Feeling;*

"Hello Dear ONES, today we wish to talk to you about cleansing and detoxing as you like t call it. We would like to ask why? Why do you feel the need to do this act once a year? We understand that you wish to feel lighter and even a little smug after indulging so much over the Christmas period.
We watch you with much humour. Why punish yourselves in such a way? The simplest way to remain in balance is oh so simple; eat light and be full of LIGHT, little and often, walk outside every day with nature, drink water and surround yourself with people who love and support you. There will be no reason to detox yourself periodically then as you naturally and quietly cleanse as part of your ritual.
Remember to cleanse yourself of people and situations too, as you grow in light and truth, spend times alone in your own company and listen to your soul calling you. There is so much more we can advise you, but for now we wish to give you this little nugget.
Sleep well dear ones and enjoy sweet dreams
as you become lighter and whole."

How very simple. Common sense too.
What do you think? Xx

17th January

Hello friends. How are you all today? Let's see what today's Get That Friday Feeling has for us;

"Welcome again Dear Ones, we look forward to our weekly meet ups and we wish to welcome some new readers today.
This little open door has been created to pass on messages to you dear reader so you can keep your faith and know that you are always surrounded and protected by angels.
Today we wish to talk to you about PLAY! Yes play. We would like you to spend more time playing, laughing, having fun so we urge
you this weekend to *go play!*
Meet with your friends and warm up the dark mornings, get out in the crisp air and skip along knowing that we are urging you, by your side. Notice how your body and emotions respond to play. Feels good eh? 'til we meet again. Your loving constant companions."

Well I know what I'm going to do this weekend. How about you dear reader, how will you play?

24th January

Good morning friends everywhere, we hope this posting finds you well today.
Did you all enjoy last Friday's message about playing? Let's hope you followed it through. So let's see what we have in store for today's Get That Friday Feeling's channelled message;

"Hello Dear friends, we meet again. We see so many of you are growing with gusto; releasing old patterns of limitations and strife. Continue we say and notice how lighter you become. Do not let life and its challenges hold you back, put your needs and desires to the forefront and join with us in your quest for happiness and fulfilment. You deserve it, all of you humans living this life have been handed an arduous task, we have it easy watching over you, trying to guide you, willing you to take the right path, make the right decision and fly with LOVE rather than fall in pain.

24th January cont.

Slow down, be still, sit in silence and breathe; the answers will come to you, your way will be illuminated. Our guidance can only come through if you open the doorway of LOVE and silence, getting though to a busy mind and continually doing is more difficult for us.
We always persevere
but if you were to be still more often
then we could work as ONE.
I am the *Archangel Of Communication*,
they call me Gabrielle. I have been a life-long friend of Angel Alison's, she saw me when her veil of illusion was down and heard me when he ears were open to receive so Dear Ones, please listen and follow these easy steps to connect and learn. We are here to LOVE,
support and guide you,
not just in your hour of need.
Be LOVE, Be still, BE AT PEACE."

24th January cont'

Oh I love these messages, I had no idea AA Gabrielle was going to come through, she WAS with me always as a child recently she gave me a nudge to say, "why don't you play with me anymore?" Think I'm going to sit and be still now to see what other messages she has.
Have a great day.
LOVE YOU xxxx

31st January

"Welcome oh welcome dear friends. We offer our LOVE and gratitude to you as you welcome in a New Year. The residue of last year will leave today with your positive intentions. It was a tough year for many which resulted in residual denseness being left in this year. So we suggest you anchor in your intention to let go of last year, the memories that caused you heart and even joy.

Let go and welcome in the new so you may fully embrace the new energetic shift of huge transformation. Letting go is key to creating a new void of energy so you may co create your life. Fill your heart with joy and positivity whilst you do this. There are a number of ways to release last year's denseness; Write a letter to it saying good bye, smudge your home and workspace with sage opening doors and windows, place an amethyst crystal in the family/relationship section of your home. Be truly present when you let go. Then simply welcome in the new with your open arms. Practice this friends and you will be in awe of what it brings unto you."

7th February

"Welcome dear hearts, as you read each post your hearts connect as ONE pulsing the great pulse of life and LOVE. Oh how much more aligned you are when you are in loving, receptive mode, open to receiving knowledge and inspiration from beings you know little about. We are everywhere; in the wind, the rain the moving of the clouds, we're in your smiles, your hearts, your schools and your wards, we are in every breath you take.

We LOVE you, we urge you to take action to be more aligned to LOVE, the place where fear is unable to reside as LOVE is far stronger. So our message for you today Dear ONE is to remove fear from your thinking just for today. When you feel a pull into the dark shadiness of your past, resist, when you choose to judge another - cease. Stop, place your hand on your heart, feel the rhythm of your beat and return to LOVE."

14th February

"Open your hearts to our presence within is our simple message to you today.
You see if you keep your hearts in love you will experience great love.
Unite your heart and mind and together we'll work as ONE.
ONE voice, ONE HEART, one LOVE"

21st February

It's Friday again, gosh it comes round so quick!

"If your life is lonely and you are sad, you have the chance to turn it around. It takes grit and determination but firstly you simply need to decide. Make that decision, trust in you then act upon your decision with YOU in mind. Taking inspired action is the way to becoming happier, healthier and whole again. Ask your-self if it is time. Time for you to transform your life into something more aligned to LOVE; moving away from fear."

*Archangel Michael through
Angel Alison Ward x*

28th February

Welcome Dear ONES, we meet again in our weekly ritual. We are so pleased you are joining us today as it is a very clear message that is important for you all to hear. The message is about communication; your inner communication.

"LISTEN to your inner guidance, listen to your inner voice. Are they conflicting or in harmony?
If your answer is conflicting then you will see and experience conflicts in your every-day life.
If this is the case here's what you do; sit down, ground, centre by breathing deeply in, holding and exhaling a few times until you're in rhythm with your breath, connect to source with your intention and heart and ask your wholeself and higher self to align in truth and love and wisdom.
You may hear or feel a click.
You will now communicate more aligned to you, your truth and your purpose both inwardly and externally. Watch how the world responds to this newly aligned state."

7th March

*Good morning angels, it's Get That Friday Feeling again; notice it's a little earlier?
I can't help but get up earlier due to
Spring-like weather here in the UK.
What's it like where you are?*

"Welcome Dear ONES, we meet again. Today we wish to keep it light and simply remind you to congratulate yourselves on your achievements, your so called failures (which are not failures at all but simply steps on your road of self discovery). Each and every one of you are applauded by us as we watch your existence on the planet earth at this time of your evolvement and personal growth.
Celebrate WHO YOU ARE, as we do,
know that you are LOVED so very, very dearly and know that we accept and understand YOU.
Today is a day where we say go shine your LIGHT to others and celebrate your LIGHT'S presence within and without... we do;
every day of your existence!"

14th March

"Welcome once again as we link in and connect via our heart space to convey our words of courage and inspiration.
For those of you at a crossroads may we suggest that you don't act straight away.
Many of you feel you have to make a quick decision then act instantly upon it. Your soul feels the uprising within and urges you to take action.
Your soul is right but it's a little eager.
Stop, place your hand on your heart and ask yourself if you chose to go the left fork in the road is this the road most favourable for you and your purpose? Or is the right road the road for you?

Taking time to connect and ask your wholeself for the best guidance surely is the best approach.

Remember Dear ONES we love you and have your best interests at heart.
Until we meet again..... BLESS YOU in your endeavours."

21st March

"Hello friends, we hope this message finds you safe and well. What is instore for YOU today?
Well hopefully if you have learnt the art of balancing your heart and mind you will create a magical and wondrous day. Allow today to be about your creations. Look from that higher place of observation and see what you have created in your life right now - without emotional attachment ideally so you can genuinely practice the gift of observation. Everyone you meet today is a mirror of you. What are they reflecting back at you.
Why not look in the mirror and see what your reflection is reflecting back at YOU!
WHAT IS YOUR FACE SAYING?
If you do not like what you see and observe what will you do? You have the tools and power to change the reflection by changing your thoughts, beliefs and actions. Remember you are a powerful being of light and freewill. You have the power to change your entire life right now, at your fingertips.
You simply have to flick the switch,
change the energy of focus and voila!
Happy reflecting dear ONES!"

28th March

"Welcome loved ones, feel our arms of love
wrap around you, letting you know
we are here, we are LOVE,
as indeed you are too.
Please remember that *YOU ARE LOVE!* Be LOVE
in all of your thoughts and actions today and
notice the difference. Be LOVE with your inner
talk and see it radiate through to others.
Be LOVE, be free!"

4th April

"Welcome again Dear Ones, today we draw your attention to your dreams.
Do you have dreams? Many of you feel that there is no point to dream, that it doesn't happen to people like you!
Well let us tell you something; *dreams happen every single moment, every single day.*
You are all deserving of enjoying seeing your dreams materialise.
So today Dear ONES, please dare to dream, know that we hear your dream
and we do respond.
You simply have to *believe* in your dreams and take action when we nudge you."

11th April

"Welcome once again dear ones as we anchor in the LIGHT to you and your planet.
It is important that you assist us at this time by releasing anything heavy, dense, unworthy or non serving. Imagine putting everything of that nature in to a giant hot air balloon and release it when full. Guard your thoughts carefully, be truthful in your mind and actions.
Walk away from others rather than stand and argue or fight. Keep yourself to yourself if you are feeling even more delicate or sensitive.
Sleep well and deeply as you find yourself in the midst of letting go on a personal layer and a global level. All will make so much more sense in the 21 days that follow.
Be kind to you and to others and you will return unscathed yet lighter. All is well."

18th April

*It's Good Friday so a very special Easter welcome to you all.
Let's see what Get That (Good) Friday Feeling has in store for us today;*

"Welcome once again as we meet as ONE. Today we ask you to explore the concept of UNITY. What does it mean to you?
Our view is that UNITY means the coming together of minds and hearts in spite of personal differences. UNITY brings your hearts and minds together as ONE for the greater good of all concerned.
We ask to contemplate UNITY today and over the weekend of Christ's upcoming and contemplate where you could unite with others for the greater good."

25th April

"Welcome Dear ONES as once again you tune in to hear our latest message to aid your growth, liberation and ascension.
We LOVE our meet-ups and urge you to continue in whatever form. Do you realise that when you have a regular meet up slot you continually build up energy, that energy is stored until you meet again and continues to grow. When one of you readers needs a little input of our LOVING energy, we zap you with it from the infinite supply this meet up has created. So Dear Ones, do not be afraid of asking for help, we urge you to reach out to another soul when in need of a boost, a hug or even words of wisdom. It is through those times that we channel our LOVE and knowledge through the person you have chosen to confide in. We work in wonderful and mysterious ways. So until next time we bid you adieu."

I do love these messages, I feel all gooey inside when they're channelled xxx enjoy your Friday xx

2nd May

"Welcome once more as we embrace you with our LOVE, wisdom and respect for living your human existence. Many people grieve when they lose someone precious to them, of course this is a human process, one that is healthy to endure but have you ever thought that maybe the loved ones who have passed see themselves as the lucky ones?

A strange thought perhaps but get this; when they go home, they are free from pain, worries of money and debt no longer haunt them and keep them awake at night, their bodies are no more as they become energy. Energy that moves and travels to wherever it wishes, they can continue with their *'earthly'* hobbies to help other souls who have passed over.

They live a life of flow and liberation and are all seeing and all knowing as they observe your life here on Earth. They *'see'* how hard living an earthly life is with all of the lessons learned, the disappointments, the ups and the downs so hear this Dear Ones, you are truly amazing, more than you will ever know.

Own up to this amazingness and be Amazing in all that you do and be-come. We LOVE you, we Honour you and we respect you..."

May 16th

*Today we welcome some new folk.
We ask them to be open to receiving
and hearing our Divine messages.*

"Today's message is all about hope. Hope is one of the core practices that keeps you all going. Hope can be found in the darkest of places, hope is given when there is nothing else to give, hope is infinite, and hope is here always.
If you need hope right now,
call upon the Angel of Hope then listen for you will hear the daintiest of music as she gracefully approaches.
Look back on your life and see when hope appeared, hope always presented itself to you even in your darkest hours when you nearly give up on her. Hope is your friend, your constant companion, hopes gives you trust!"

May 23rd

"Welcome Dear ONES as we gather in the LIGHT TO YOU today. We bring the LIGHT in many forms, sun shine, warmth from your heart or another's,
laughter, joy and compassion.
You, as you well know are made up of both LIGHT and shadow. Sometimes the light will show up your shadow side;
if you are brave enough to acknowledge it, it too will be shown light, releasing the density from the egoic associated feelings and subsequent actions.
So the next time you are aware
of your shadow side,
don't hide it away.
Look at what it is showing you, acknowledge it and allow the LIGHT to enter....
let us know how you get on.
We're always with you."

May 30th

"Today we welcome you once more and wish to talk about trust. When trust leaves a relationship, the relationship breaks down.
How do you re-build trust?
As always it has to start with you; remember your relationships are reflected aspects of yourself, so if someone shows you distrust or their behaviour is untrustworthy what is that saying of you?
Think about it before answering...
There is some aspect of you, that YOU do not trust! Be it your decision making, your listening to guidance whatever! If you are really honest you will find it, look at it, listen to it and bring trust back into your life - your relationships will soon reflect this new level of trust.
Of course there will be goodbyes too but this is significant as you're not saying their behaviour (and yours) is acceptable."

June 6th

Dear ONES, when you open your heart and balance your mind, you open yourself to many opportunities. The door of your inner communication opens allowing you to listen to your own counsel and fly.
So then why do you seek others' counsel when you are in a dilemma?
You have all the answers within YOU.
All you need to do to access these answers is to sit, ground, centre and ask the question whilst waiting patiently for the response!
Try it and report to us your successes.

June 13th

Welcome once more Dear Ones as we cross the void between being human and
the greater consciousness.
We love our meet ups and know they help heal you on a deep level. Knowledge gives you wisdom and strength and that's where we would like to stay today in the knowledge that you dear ONE, the person reading this is safe, LOVED and valued. Your outer world may not be showing that right now but let us reassure you that you are safe, all is well. Remember to stay out of your dramas that you have created, it keeps you stuck in the mire.
Learn from what has occurred with honest conviction and move on in the knowledge that you have learned something new about you, then simply forgive. Knowledge is power but it is power-less if you do not acknowledge what you have learnt.

June 20th

Welcome once more Dear ONES as we bring a ray of LIGHT and LOVE into all you readers. We are aware of the heaviness residing in many of you at the moment. This could be from old hurts, current stresses, expectations and unhappiness that life is not going how you planned it. Let go of these hurts on the wave of the Solstice energy through offering the residual lower energy to us so we may transmute it. Create your very own letting go and releasement ceremonies as you intend to clear yourself. By releasing such density you will become lighter in feeling and thinking which as you now know will create lighter,
LOVE based behaviours which then in turn create healthy habits.
If you need help, ask your mentor to assist you. A trusted wise soul who encourages you to take a look into your life without attachment, judgement and criticism.
If you haven't got a mentor then ask us to assist you find one. Stay LIGHT!

June 27th

Dear ONES we call you in today to create your own prayer circles not only to those in need but also to those of you who are in a great place right now.
The mixture of the energy vibrations will enhance the groups' vibration bringing balance and equinox.
Resist the temptation to focus on the problem; it says you do not believe in a resolution. Simply state the positive prayer, join as ONE, ONE group = ONE voice and rest assured, we hear you, we see you, we LOVE YOU.
Until we meet again...

July 4th

When the truth is shown, it is shown the light to be healed and dissipated into the ether. Many of you are afraid of truth, whether it is purely giving your honest opinion or simply stating what your heart is saying. Do not fear Dear ONE for when the truth is born, there is no going back to those dark places of fearful communication with oneself and others. To speak ones truth is living a life based on LOVE, purpose in true authenticity. As soon as you make the switch it will become easier. Our LOVE is with you Dear ONES in this time of finding TRUTH. Remember, it starts with you."